Bianca C. Ross

Herbert Peabody

and How Food Finds Your Fork

Illustrated by Tabitha Emma Bray

Published in Australia by Halsbury Co
First published in Australia in 2020
© Text copyright 2020, Bianca C. Ross
© Design and Illustration copyright Halsbury Co
Herbert Peabody ® is a registered trademark of Halsbury Co
Printed in Australia by Ingram Spark

Contact details: hello@herbertpeabody.com

Website: www.herbertpeabody.com

Cover design, typesetting: Tabitha Emma Bray

The right of Bianca C. Ross to be identified as the Author of the Work has been asserted in accordance with the Copyright, Designs and Patents Act 1988.
This book is a work of fiction.
Any similarities to that of people living or dead are purely coincidental.
All rights reserved. No part of this publication may be reproduced, stored in a retrieval system, or transmitted, in any form or by any means without the prior written permission of the publisher, nor be otherwise circulated in any form of binding or cover other than that in which it is published and without a similar condition being imposed on the subsequent purchaser.
Ross, Bianca C.
Herbert Peabody
ISBN: 978-0-6487847-3-9
pp 22

This book is for those who believe being curious is wonderful!

This is Herbert Peabody.

He is a farmer.

This is Herbie's big vegetable patch where he grows vegetables.

Can you see what Herbie is growing?

What colour are the pumpkins?

Can you count the pumpkins?

Today, Herbie is picking the pumpkins to deliver to the greengrocer.

Can you help him find the pumpkins to pick?

Herbie drives his truck into town to deliver the pumpkins to the greengrocer.

The greengrocer puts the pumpkins on the shelf.

People go to the greengrocer to buy fruit and vegetables.

They love to buy Herbie's pumpkins.

And they love to take them home and eat them!

This is how food comes from the farm and finds your fork.

The End

BOOKS IN THE HERBERT PEABODY SERIES

Picture Books

Herbert Peabody and The Funky Fruit Book

Herbert Peabody and The Edgy Veggie Book

Herbert Peabody and The Friendly Friends Book

Herbert Peabody and How Food Finds Your Fork

Herbert Peabody and The Magic Seeds

Chapter Books with Pictures

Herbert Peabody and His Extraordinary Vegetable Patch

Herbert Peabody and The Incredible Beehive

E-cookbooks

Herbert Peabody Kids Cookbook Easter Food

Herbert Peabody Kids Cookbook Christmas Food

Herbert Peabody Kids Cookbook Food to Share

And head to www.herbertpeabody.com for your FREE downloads and activities.

Bianca C. Ross

Tabitha Emma Bray

Bianca C. Ross is the biographer for Herbert Peabody, the farmer helping children grow in a happy and healthy world. With a global career in research, marketing and advertising, Bianca understands Herbie's need to help people reconnect with their food and community, and show children how this can be done in a fun way.

Herbie lives on Mulberry Tree Farm in Huffelton. Bianca lives in Melbourne, Australia.

Tabitha Emma Bray's career in graphic design and illustration spans over a decade. Her passion for making and creating began when she was a young girl, and now her stunning designs and illustrations feature in the Herbert Peabody children's book series, as well as other commercial design projects.

Tabitha lives in Orange, Australia, with her husband and two young boys.

www.ingramcontent.com/pod-product-compliance
Lightning Source LLC
Chambersburg PA
CBHW041429010526
44107CB00045B/1551